C000301753

this is my song

*tanka prose
about letting go, letting be*

Joy McCall

Keibooks
Perryville, Maryland, USA
2019

this is my song

tanka prose about letting go letting be

Joy McCall

Copyright 2019 by Joy McCall

All rights reserved. No part of this book may be reproduced in any form or by any means, except by a reviewer or scholar who may quote brief passages in a review or article.

Cover copyright 2019 "The Ford, Norfolk, England" by Peter Bromage. Used with permission.

ISBN-13: 978-1073513109 (Print)

Available in print and Kindle.

Keibooks
P O Box 346
Perryville, MD 21903
http://AtlasPoetica.org
Keibooks@gmail.com

Acknowledgements

Many of these tanka prose pieces previously appeared in *Atlas Poetica, Bamboo Hut, Bright Stars, Haibun Today, Ribbons,* and *Skylark.* The editors' kind acceptances are greatly appreciated.

this is my story
this is my song . . .

from a hymn by blind poet Frances Jane Crosby
New York City, 1873

to Andy, Kate and Wendy
with love

Table of Contents

introduction

All Journeys Start with a Dream

In the eight years since Joy McCall first submitted her tanka poetry to me at *Atlas Poetica,* I have seen her grow and expand as a poet while still maintaining a clear sense of self and personal style. Perhaps it is an advantage of age and experience. By the time she began publishing tanka poetry, she was already – if I may use an archaic word – a crone. She knew who she was and what she valued, and that appears implicitly and explicitly in her poetry. Although she has questions, *Is there a God?* and *What happens after we die?* these are philosophical questions, not questions of personal identity. When she speaks of herself as minnow, deer, hedgewitch, or wheelchair user, these are all manifestations of her reality. Indeed, many of her tanka prose pieces take place in an imaginary world and are peopled with characters both real and unreal.

Dreams are frequent topics for poets, but few handle them with the skill that Joy does. That is because for most poets, dreams are unreal, imaginary experiences, but for Joy, they are lived experiences. When she speaks of camping in a cave, we don't know if this is taking place in the material world or the immaterial world. Joy travels both planes of existence at will. We know that when she had her motorcycle, she often visited remote places, camping out, and meeting strangers. Even in her wheelchair, she finds people that will carry her to places she wishes to go. Sometimes they are friends and family and sometimes they are strangers. Thus, when we find her on a moor in the company of a taciturn Gypsy, we don't know if it is a current

13

event, a memory, or a dream. It is Joy's great gift that she can simultaneously experience the overlapping planes of reality: present, past, and possible.

Joy has the peculiar effect on people that, living or dead, they decide to speak to her. Whether a tattooed woman sitting down to write tanka with her at a cafe table, a blind man asking her to describe the night sky, or a ghost drifting up out of the earth to compliment her for the music, or the crooks (offenders and ex-offenders) who build, fix, and carry for her, she is as likely to be found having a conversation with a rabbi as a homeless man. Children and dead people confide their secrets to her, and so do witches, madwomen, criminals, and whores. Joy passes no judgments. All are human beings to her, each with their own stories, their own pain, their own demons, and their own gifts. Joy's gift to all of us is her ability to open the door between the planes so that we too can step through and experience the world as she experiences it, conveyed to us through the medium of tanka and prose.

this is my song is a collection of tanka prose pieces: pieces that combine prose with poetry. This type of prosimetrum is ancient in Japan, going back to the poetic diaries and the headnotes accompanying the earliest tanka poems. Joy is telling us the stories of her life and the lives of those she meets, elevated through the use of poetic language to illuminate the light within even the darkest places. Arranged in the form of a spiritual journey, the pieces progress naturally from the curiosity, optimism, and rebellion of starting out, to the encounters along the way, to the dangers and detours that complicate the path, to way stations of solace and restoration, to at last arrive at the unknown destination.

All destinations are unknown. Whatever we may expect, once we arrive, they are never exactly as we thought they would be. Yet if we open ourselves to let go and let be, we discover something we never knew we needed until it found us. It is a privilege to accompany Joy on her journey, both in the material world and the world of poetry. If you have read Joy's books before, then you know what to expect, but whatever you are imagining, it will be different. If you have never read Joy's work before, then you are in for a treat as she takes you to the hidden places of our world that lie within plain sight, but are unseen by ordinary eyes. This is Joy's song, and we are lucky she has chosen to share it with us.

M. Kei
June 2019

the journey begins

bats and vespers

It was an old convent just outside Toronto – the Sisters of Saint Joseph – standing in vast grounds; a quiet place away from the city noise and lights; tall trees, wide lawns, curving driveways, heavy gates.

One of the wings of the building was set aside as a hospice for old, ill, and dying nuns and monks.

I worked as the night nurse there. Monks and nuns, just like Ryokan, like all of us, need loving human care when they grow frail.

There was a high-roofed chapel next to the sick bay and I would hear the chanting of vespers, of late compline, of vigils, of lauds.

the echoes
of chanted prayers
hung on the air
the holiness, the quietness
the gentle peace

When a patient was dying I would wake a young monk or a nun to come and sit at the bedside to pray until the last breath, and a while after.

Sometimes the patients had old age dementia and all the years of strict daily discipline would be lost.

There was a sweet kind of humanity in those folk.

One old nun loved to dance in the moonlight.

out on the lawn
under the moon
she danced
her long white gown
brushing the grass

A little while of dancing and I would take her hand for a few more turns and then dance her indoors to her bed and she would sleep, content.

There were a few nights when the patients all slept (no tiresome bureaucracy and form-filling in those days) and I would sit and read between making rounds – usually poetry, sometimes old novels.

the ghosts
of long-dead monks
and nuns
slipping through the trees
there – and then gone

Bats would fly up and down the corridors, with that uncanny sense of direction they have, hearing echoes of their own voices.

bat wings
just above my head
ruffling my hair
that eerie feeling
something primal, ancient

I wonder why a person would choose to be a nun or a monk. There seem to be many reasons, not just for the religion.

It is a safe and secure way of living, among like-minded people, sheltered from the outside world with all its beauty and despair.

It would not be my way.

I like my life
in all the colours
of the rainbow
not for me the monochrome
of holy orders

As Oodgeroo of the Nunuccal tribe wrote in her poem 'Song' —

Grief is not in vain
It's for our completeness.
If the fates ordain
Love to bring life sweetness,
Welcome too its pain.

sayings

My mum was a woman of old sayings, like her mother before her: 'Don't upset the apple cart,' she said – but I did.

I tipped over
the apple cart
laughing
as the creatures came
feasting in the gutters

She said, 'Make hay while the sun shines' and 'get out of the kitchen, child – too many cooks spoil the broth' and 'don't dig up the gold, let it lie' and 'don't count your chickens until they are hatched.'

My stern father's favourite saying was, 'Spare the rod and you'll spoil the child.' I was in no danger of spoiling.

My mother countered that with, 'Do unto others as you would have them do unto you' and 'never look a gift horse in the mouth' . . . and 'a stitch in time saves nine' . . .

I changed that one to –

when the cloth
is worn thin
it is time
to buy yourself
a new apron

My laughing English grandfather's sayings made no sense at all — 'Why is a mouse when it spins? The higher, the fewer.'

My serious Swedish grandfather said — 'To get to heaven, child, don't stray from the straight and narrow road' — and so I —

I wandered
over the green hills
and far away
and all the sayings
followed me, grumbling, scolding

shanties

I was thinking about all the sailors I have seen heading out to sea from the shores of Canada and America and England, Scotland, Wales and Ireland and Norway and Sweden and all the coastal places I have been;

and I was hearing sea shanties in my head;

and then I remembered the old harbour master on the north Wales coast at Abergele, who used to bless the boats as they came and went out to the Irish Sea.

I remember what he used to say, waving his lantern —

fair winds
and following seas
bless the sailors
heading out onto the water
at the mercy of time and tides

and I remember the little 5th century church the old sailors went to worship, (and in the end, to be laid to rest) when they were too frail to go to sea anymore —

St. Cynfran
patron saint of cattle
and the land
son of Brychan Brycheiniog
the ancient lord

and besides the sea shanties in my head, I hear the Welsh children singing the *Canu Plygam,* the *Pulli Cantus* *

dark Christmas morning
the sun not risen
the cock crows
the children sing
the fifteen holy songs

* Latin for cock crow

and all this music, and the breaking waves, and the rush of the wind, are sounding, ringing, and what else matters now, but the song of the sea in my head?

chance encounters

Calling for a boiler service, after a long wait I get a young lad called Danny with a singsong Welsh accent and instead of gas supply, we speak of the Rhondda valleys and the closing of all the coal mines and his longing to make art and design and roam singing in the fields of his native south Wales, instead of working in a noisy London office with a dozen others, answering phones for a huge company.

life is not
what he expected
or wanted
he does a job he hates
to pay the rent

I tell him
just begin —
one step
onto the path
you long for

there are many ways
to reach a dream
a quick jump
or a long winding road
with light up ahead

in the end
we forget the boiler
I go to write poems
he goes to write down
one step towards his own light

Now the boiler is still broken, and I have to spend an age on the phone again, trying to get connected to an engineer.

autumn

someone asked me my favourite colour and the muse
began to sing – and now I'm hoping other poets will sing
their songs, too –

beech leaves
holding on all winter
hazelnuts, acorns
the doe asleep
on fallen leaves

oak leaves
thick on the ground
where the mouse hides
berberis leaves
in wintertime

café mocha
caramel fudge
curry sauce
cumerin, turmeric
ginger, cinnamon, cloves

tree sap
ancient amber
firelight
candle flame
the sunset sky

peanut butter
mandarin oranges
marmalade
the soft feathers of chickens
the eyes of owls

orange calcite
carnelian
smoky quartz
sunstone, tiger-eye
jasper yellow and red

golden pine
wicker baskets
saffron threads
foxes and their cubs
bay horses, brown cows

chutney
carrot soup
honey
maple syrup
brown sugar

beeswax
bee pollen
catkins
sweet potatoes
worn bricks

old rum
Tennessee whisky
my quilt
old oak floors
my favourite sweater

Joy McCall

ochre
burnt umber
sepia
russet, raw sienna
oh . . . autumn

Joey's Word

the little boy
sits on an old milking stool
at the foot of my bed
while I read him stories
from my own childhood

Sometimes it's a poem by A. A. Milne — he likes those best. I have to read *'The King's Breakfast'* at least once a week —

the king asked the queen
and the queen asked
the dairymaid
could we have some butter
for the royal slice of bread? . . .

The little boy would like to be a King as he could have anything he wants and not have to go to school, as he will next year.

Yesterday, after I read a poem, he stood up, hands on his hips and said, 'I will read you a story tomorrow.'

I said, 'Do you know how to read already?' He said —

I cannot read yet
but if an old woman
like you
can do it, I can do it
in a flash!

Today he wandered down the lane again and stood by my
bed and said —

this reading thing
is not as easy
as I thought it would be
maybe you are
quite smart

I said, 'When you go to school you will be reading as
quick as a wink.'

'But I want to read you a story now,' he said, sadly.

I said, 'Why don't you make one up until you learn to
read?'

He pondered that for a moment and then he said, very
excited, 'Then it would be MY story, right? And we could
put it in a real book?'

'Yes, we could,' I said, and he began —

there was
an old woman
with white hair
she was so old
she was almost dead

she was
quite smart
because
she knew how
to read real books

there was a Boy
who was also smart
and soon
he will be able to read
very important books

the Boy
when he can read
will be going
on a big adventure
into space

the old woman
will look up
as he flies away
and she will wave
and cry

the Boy
will bring a present
for her
from space
when he comes back

maybe a star
or a dinosaur
or a dead alien
or some sun dust
or a firefly

Joey sighed, 'I don't know what to bring you. You only like reading, except trees and birds and they don't have them in space.'

I said, 'What about bringing me a word from space? I love words.'

He was quiet for a while, then he said, 'I will bring you the very best word; but I haven't thought of it yet.'

he turned to go home
and at the door he stopped
and shouted –
I will bring you
the word FIRE!

'That's a fine word,' I said. 'I like it.'

'Yes,' he said. 'I see you by the fire every day in your holy room when I am going up the stairs to bed; and you could have a FIRE tattoo, with flames.'

And I thought, 'Actually, yes, I could.'

I wrote
the word FIRE
in big letters
on a sheet of paper
and gave it to him

He said ,'FIRE.' I said, 'Yes.' He laughed – 'See, I told
you I can learn to read in a flash.'

    and he went out
    across the lane
    waving the paper in the air
    saying over and over again
    Fire! Fire! Fire!

impossible love

The small girl curled up on the foot of my bed wrapped up in a quilt this cold morning, is listening as I read, 'The Monk and the Mermaid.'*

She has been curious about mermaids for much of her ten years, but knows nothing of monks so I explain their strange ways.

by Kenneth Steven

I have to explain the new (to her) meaning of 'habits.'

the monks
in their habits
chanting
vespers—
she grows sleepy

As we get into the book she wakes more, sits up and looks carefully at all the illustrations.

She was not sure what a monk looked like but the mermaid is just as she thought.

she wonders
if there are mermaids
in the Norfolk Broads
I say—*who knows?*
anything is possible

Her brown eyes widen when I get to the bit about the loving friendship between the monk and the mermaid having to come to an end.

the mermaid
is bound to the salt
of the sea
the monk is bound
to his habit

Eddi sits bolt upright and looks serious. 'I shall never fall in love with a monk,' she says, 'that kind of thing is nothing but heartbreak.'

I ask her what kind of boy she might love. (I was thinking that when I was ten I had never thought of love. Today's kids grow up too soon).

She ponders a while. Then she says, 'I will love someone like Ed Sheeran, unless I am a mermaid by then'.

Fair enough, at least Ed is a local boy.

encounters

sheepfold

I parked the motorbike against the wall of a broken-down hut, halfway up a small hill. A little further up the gentle slope there were a few grazing sheep near a dry stone sheepfold that had seen better days. It was full of grass and weeds and it seemed a long time since sheep had been there.

I sat inside, set down my helmet and took food and water from my backpack. Leaning against the broken wall, I felt the stones' warmth from the day's sun. It had been a long day's ride. I must have fallen asleep sitting there, sheltered from the wind, in the peace and quiet of the hills. When I woke, it was dark and three sheep had come into the fold and settled for the night.

something
so comforting
about sheep
the thick wool
the gentle baa

No wonder the good book mentions sheep and shepherds so often. These old sheep with no shepherd, just living out their days on the hills.

I did not mean
to spend the night there
but . . . the sheep
the hill fold
the sky full of stars

Sometimes if we listen, life holds out its hand to us, saying: look, I'm giving you this . . . do you see it?

It was just like that.

the stars
the shelter of the fold
the sheep
the long grasses
the night breezes

When I woke, they had gone, ambling down the hill. I could see my red bike still leaning against the broken hut. Although everything looked the same as when I came – the sheep, the fold, the grassy hill, the old hut – something inside me was changed.

you sit by the fire
watching the flames
for so long
you feel yourself filled
with hearthfire light

roads less travelled

So there's a place I go as often as I can, to the small hill where the ruins of the Viking church still stand. It's a quiet place where solitude comes easy. The little roads around are definitely the roads less travelled.

Still they have their stories to tell.

Roger's Lane

centuries ago
in the old village pub
there was a landlord
his name was Roger
he was a dour-faced man

he was mean
with the pints of ale
mean with the potatoes
mean with his tired
down-trodden wife

one winter day
in a fit of temper
he killed a man
who owed him coins
for old ale

so the lane
which led to the pub
was given his name
even as he himself
hung on the gallows

and it is still
Roger's Lane
though he is bones
and his crime
long since forgotten

Hollow Lane

there were
five churches once
in this small hamlet
all the villagers
faithful worshippers

times passed
and religion failed
those common people
and they stopped trailing
up the hill in their Sunday best

one by one
the bored priests left
for pastures new
the old churches
fell into disrepair

the road that once
was named Holy Lane
gave up its ghost
and the villagers
called it Hollow

two churches
still welcome
the faithful few
the others lie in ruins
lost in thickets and brambles

Hawes Green

once there was a place
on the hill outside
the old village
a place of escape of sorts
a place of sin

the cheap whores
gathered there
in the ruins
of the old sanitarium
where the lepers' bones lie

after dark
the men would climb the hill
husbands, drunks
farm workers
even the odd priest

it was not
a happy place
the women were poor
and ill and weary
and the men discontented

one by one the whores
died and were buried
in the churchyards
and the Whores' Green
got a nice new name

when I wander those old roads up the hill and pass the thickets where old churches stood, I pass the lane that leads to the ruins of the ancient priory of St. Botolph, now a farm and stables. Sometimes I turn aside from the hill and go along the lane with the grass growing up the middle. There are fields of rape and barley on either side. It's a peaceful place where the wind blows much of the time over the open land from the sea. Halfway along the lane there's a turning, mostly hidden in gorse and tall grasses. There's an old fence there, overgrown with ivy and blackberry thorns. Beside the brambles is the cracked road sign – Sluts' Hole Lane.

No doubt, one day, it will change its name too but I hope not. There's a charm of sorts in places and their names.

the moon, Venus and the bus stop

I was sitting outside in my wheelchair at dusk, looking up to the sky to see the crescent moon and a new sighting of the bright planet Venus.

A young man waiting at the bus stop at our door said, 'Hello, do you need to pass by?'

I explained about the sky and the moon and the planet; and he said, 'oh, please tell me how it looks?'

And then I saw the white cane, the dark glasses. So I said,

the moon
is a curved crook, I can see
the earthlight shadow
and Venus is a bright light
low down near the horizon

and I said —

up to the east
Orion is leaning back
facing the moon
the three stars in his belt
glittering in a row

He smiled. I asked him how he would know when the bus was coming. He replied, 'I'm going to the hospital, to visit my love. When I hear a bus coming around the corner

47

(they sound different from trucks and vans and cars) I stop it by waving my white stick and I ask where they are going. The drivers never seem to mind stopping to tell me, even when I don't get on board. They are kind.'

He asked me, 'Why are you in a wheelchair? I heard it coming up the lane.' I told him of the crash and the paralysis.
He said, 'I hear suffering when you speak,' and I said, 'and I hear sadness in your voice.'
So we spoke of sorrow and frustration and loss, and whether to be unable to see is any worse than to be unable to walk and stand.

    we both wept
    at the bus stop
    in the cold dusk
    under the streetlight
    under the moon and stars

    and I sat
    and he stood
    and we held hands
    in the bus shelter
    until the right bus came

and he waved goodbye, and Venus slid below the horizon and the moon set and I went indoors to sit by the fire, and life slipped back to what passes for normal here on Dales Place.

blessed be

for Carole and Kathryn

They came from America, two old poet-friends, to walk on my small East Anglian fields.

We felt like Shakespeare's three witches with the cold wind blowing our hair, and the wide skies dark and threatening rain.

the Archer
oak lover, tattoo'd *enough,*
the graveyard Goat
bemused by the dark yew,
the Fish in the thin stream

All around us were the signs of history going far back in time, stopping now and then leaving way-markers at shifting points — the Viking intruders, the Roman invaders, the Anglo-Saxons, the Iceni tribes, the early Christians, the ages of bronze and iron and stone . . . and a sense of the timeless, back to the Dawn.

Are there ghosts? Do all men, all creatures, leave the marks of their being on the air, on the land, in the waters?

We three felt it, there on the desolate bitter hill.

Joy McCall

the cold wind howled
on the Iceni hill
black rooks rose
from Viking pines
a bay horse stood alone

hawthorn hedgerows
heavy with red berries
edged the narrow lanes
that wound through green fields . . .
and above, the wide dark skies

it was a time
of gathering – pebbles
tales, imaginings
lichened sticks, visions,
fallen oak leaves

old stories
lay all around us
Roman cart tracks
Iceni chariot ruts
the echoes of battle

we were witches
taking strange shapes
on the low hill
the wind blew wild
through our aged hair

minnows

In the hill woods there's a clear rippling stream. I spend a long time on the bank watching the water.

On the far bank there are seven birds picking in the damp earth, getting worms. I don't know this kind of bird — they are small and very dark.

I'm sitting under a tree. A school of silver minnows is swimming fast upstream.

the water
ripples
with light
and shade
and splashes

There are too many minnows to count, though I love counting.

I watch their hurry as they swim, sometimes darting around rocks and through reeds.

They come to a deeper slower part of the stream.

they rest there
a while, moving slowly
circling
as if they were gathering
strength for the journey

Then as one, the great busy school swims fast upstream
and out of my sight.
    I sit longer, watching the dark birds.
    An otter comes out from the reeds.

    I love minnows. They are brave, bright, small silver fish.
    If I lived in these woods, that's what I would be.
    Or perhaps an otter. or a dark bird on the bank.
    Or the tree I sit under.
    Perhaps even . . . myself

the ford

There are two old men crossing a ford where the shallow stream runs over the road. It is evening and the sky is almost dark. One man is carrying an oil lantern. It doesn't give much light. Perhaps, enough. They are talking quietly. They have known each other a very long time.

The stream bed is slippery. The older man stumbles. His friend puts out his hand and steadies him. 'Remember when we drank so much of that rare whiskey that we fell down in the pub garden and slept there until the landlord woke us, at noon the next day?'

they laugh
there is a beauty
in quiet friendship
and a kind of trust
that only comes with time

more limpet than woman

Limpet — from Old English lempedu — 'to lick the stone'.

"Cheer up, as the limpet said to the weeping willow" —
Edward Lear

while the waters
of the great sea
wash over her
the common limpet
clings to the rock

When limpets are fully clamped down, it is impossible to remove them from the rock using brute force alone. The limpet will allow itself to be destroyed rather than stop clinging to its rock.

As hard times and high waves come, I too hide in the shell and stick to the rock.

the limpet
has but one leg
to creep
across the rocks
slowly, slowly

the limpet
has a beating heart
vesicles and veins
its half-hidden eye
sees light and dark

its scores
of teeth like iron
scrape the rock
eating algae
vegan, like me

when the seas
were first parted
from the land
the limpet was there
clinging, dreaming

somehow they know
the time, the seasons
all the limpets
letting go their gifts
of egg and sperm

I would gather
the empty shells
at the tideline
and make a necklace
for myself

I would pray
to the limpet gods
help me cling
to heartbeat and rock
while the waves crash

Joy McCall

I have one leg
and a hidden eye
and I know
the changing of the seasons
the time for loving

I am common
like the limpet
and I am stubborn . . .
in the heaviness
of time and tide I cling

encounter

I'm sitting at a pavement cafe in the darker, grittier part of old Norwich, drinking coffee and reading poetry.

A young woman comes up and asks what I'm reading.

I say, 'tanka,' a bit annoyed at being disturbed.

She asks, 'Whose tanka?'

I look up, stunned, surprised that anyone in this backwoods place would even know the word tanka.

She is very thin but beautiful, with long mahogany-red hair. She wears heavy silver chain bracelets.

The thing that strikes me is the tattoos. Her arms and legs are covered in fine black lines, gaelic words and celtic designs and small bits of poetry. I offer to buy her a coffee. She says, 'Throw in lunch, I'm hungry.' So I do.

We are sitting under an awning and it is raining lightly. Then the sun comes out. There's a double rainbow over the Cathedral and the Castle.

The young woman eats, saying little. I go on reading. Then she says, 'Write with me – you begin'. So I write:

lady, the earth calls
whispering low
seductive
saying come, come,
I am your mother

I don't know where that came from – picking up something from her eyes, or her tattoos maybe.

She begins to cry, and writes:

my mother
is long long-dead
she cannot
hurt me now, I rise
a wild woman, a goddess

She watches my face as I read the poem. I ask her: 'Shall we stop?'
She does not speak but writes again :

I will cover
my skin in words
and signs
I want no kindred ink
mixed with my blood

She reaches across the table and rests her hand on mine. On each of her thin fingers, there's a tattoo word. I read :

there's
no
way
home

I take the pen and write :

home is illusion
and paradox
it is within
where the fire burns
and there is bread

She leans across the table and touches my hair. She takes the pen and the tanka book (both mine), and walks away. I didn't even ask her name. I wish I had. She didn't ask mine.

poison trees

The ley line I am following comes to an abrupt end where the land meets the sea.

There is a small island not far from the shore. I find an old boatman in the village who will take me there.

He says he will return for me at the end of the day. It will be five pounds each way. I wonder about that.

He parks my old motorbike in his lean-to shed.

the island
is heavy with trees
the green gods
grow wild here
I kneel at their feet

The trees are strange ones to find on an island.

I think about the Nordic boat-builders. They used these three woods, dovetailed, for the hulls of their boats.

One kind of wood on its own would crack apart and the boat would sink.

They named the juniper *communis* for it must have the company of other trees.

I wonder if they came here once, long ago.

the boughs
carry the poison
'woman's ruin'
the common juniper
the rowan, the twisted yew

The leaves of these trees are deadly food for man and beast.

Too many juniper berries in the gin will cause a woman to miscarry and die.

The island is silent except for the distant cries of seagulls and the faint wash of waves.

> thick moss
> grows on thin bones
> held fast
> in the slow grip
> of twisted roots

> someone before me
> chewed the leaf
> tasted the berry . . .
> will I too, die gin-drunk
> under the savage trees?

Overcome with weariness, I lie down. My head is full of old poems from my Sami ancestors:

. . . the smoke from our fires drives away the herd . . . let us eat the dry meat in the tents, let us make love, and sleep . . .

> smitten
> by the low song
> of the night-wind
> I sleep, like the dead
> beneath the dark triad

Crazy Eva

I used to ride the motorbike on my day off into the countryside and would meet all kinds of strange Norfolk people, peasants really.

I often went by a ruined house and thought no one lived there until I saw her one day — and went back several times to see her again, in case she needed a friend.

She got used to the sound of the bike and would come scowling to the door. I never went close as it was clear callers were not welcome.

I did leave a box of chocolates and some tangerines on the path once. I don't know if she ate them.

The landlord at the pub where I had lunch told me about her. He said that her parents owned the great house but they grew old and died and she was broke and so the house fell to ruin but she lived on alone there in one room. He thought she had no relatives. No one came to see her. The people of the village just called her Crazy Eva.

> she looked like a witch
> wild long grey hair
> filthy ragged clothes
> tall and bony
> bent and aged

I wished
she was happy
living like that
and not lonely
but who knows?

They found her long-dead a few years after my crash and
the house has been demolished, although the old ivied walls
around the plot still stand.

I don't know where she is buried but it would be a
pauper's grave. If I knew where, I would take flowers.

I wrote this for her, long ago, while sitting on my old
bike in the lane that passed her house.

Crazy Eva
she lives on cornflakes
boxes and boxes
piled in the corners
of her dirty room

Crazy Eva
lives in a derelict house
dutch gables
and potted orchids
at the front door

Crazy Eva
her garden is a forest
hidden behind a wall
covered in ivy
and creepers

Crazy Eva
she only comes out at night
all day she wanders
muttering, around
the crumbling rooms

Crazy Eva
the village boys
call her a witch
and throw stones
in her well

Crazy Eva
who could love her?
I think I do . . .

on Barton Fell

The motorbikes were parked way down the hill, in the little Cumbrian village.

We climbed the long rough track, where Romans once drove their carts, up towards the mountains.

It was a desolate place in the winter, and we saw no other travellers there.

We planned to go further but stopped as the snowfall grew heavy, and took night shelter in a neolithic cave.

steady all day and night
the snow had been falling
the supper-fire went out
it was dark and cold
in the shallow cave

The hill ponies, small and black, were restless. They stirred, standing under the sparse hawthorns, waiting for the sunrise.

Once a pony had fallen down into an ancient fire-pit and died there, and some long-ago people had laid it out, all straight.

When we came there, the body was bones, disturbed a little by something digging, perhaps a fox.

we thought to cover the body
and say some prayers
but then, the wind
and the winter snows
were sacrament enough

The nearby Cockpit stone circle sits half-buried in earth, the capstone aligned with a distant hill where beacons once flared to show the way.

The Roman cart track leads past the ruins of the neolithic settlement, away into the hills, and disappears in fallen rocks.

It is a strange, unearthly kind of place. I sensed the spirits of those ancient people, still dwelling there among the rocks and stones.

we slept awhile,
and did I dream
the ancient guttural voices :
'what people are these,
so thin, their skin so pale?'

the straight road to yarmouth

the old mill
without roof and sails,
home to bats
a sad kind of place
slowly derelict

Ramblers have trodden a path past the broken front door on their way to the sea. There are no houses in sight.

the salt wind blows
across the marshes
all year long
eroding the mortar
stunting the wild reeds

The straight road between the wetlands is bordered by ditches that run with water. The ruined mill breaks the monotony of bare landscape.

cows shelter
from the driving rain
on the west side,
a tramp stumbles inside
seeking a place to sleep

He settles heavily, against a crumbling brick oven. A charred thigh bone falls at his side.
He sleeps like the dead all night, muttering.

Mazed Kate

Dreaming of the moors, I stumble across the witch again.
She is still mazed as a stoat.

She spends her nights sleeping curled close to the small
wild ponies, huddling against them for warmth.

she wanders all day
in wind and rain
gathering
blackthorns and thistles
hawthorn leaves and berries

she knows
the magic of potions
she watches
creatures in the moonlight
and learns their names

she finds
fallen branches
that suit her
for making wands
and pendants

She is growing older and I worry about her, living wild on
the cold winter moor, at the mercy of the elements and evil-
doers and trips and falls.

She laughs — *What better place could there be to end my
days?*

for a hedgewitch
to die by her night fire
warmed by the body
of a sleeping animal
is the way it should be

I send her blackberry wine for Yule. She will warm it in the battered pot on her fire, and drink it all and sleep and dream a new spell.

I send her
good rough blankets
she lays them
on the shivering foals
in the cold nights

I knit for her
warm red woolen mittens
she uses them
to gather acorns
and hazelnuts

I have learned to send her bags made of sacking with long handles; and pencils and paper for writing, and coins for the phone.

the weather is harsh
on the southern moors
her life is hard
and oh how I wish
it was mine . . . mine

hope and cedar leaves

I'm sitting with my back against the rough bark of a tree.
There are cedars and Douglas Firs and apple trees in
this corner of the field.
Small apples lie on the ground.
He picks one up, and takes a bite. It is mealy and tart.
He says *we will come back and pick apples when they
are ripe on the tree.*

my heart sings
a song of time
stretching out
of fir cones, and apples
hope and cedar leaves

dark, light, shade

The hot summer air is heavy with the smell of slurry. The harvests are done and now the farmers spread pig shit to feed the ground for next year's crops.

my heart aches
the pig fields are empty
the abattoir
fills with the sounds
of slaughter

School is out and the families head for the coast. Children build sandcastles and swim and eat ice cream. A whale lies dead on a local beach. It has swallowed dozens of bits of plastic.

plastic washes up
on every shore
the tides bring
man's waste
back to haunt us

Wildfires are blazing all over Europe, Scandinavia, Canada, all over the world. Even some small Norfolk cornfields are on fire.

Joy McCall

the English streams
and ponds are dry
dead fish
litter the riverbeds
the land is parched

I weep all night. It does no good.

on the telephone wire
above the factory
a greenfinch is singing
its wheezy
one-note summer song

everything

I'm dreaming, wandering through an old evergreen forest of pine and fir and cedar. It's a warm day.

The sunlight is shining through the leaves and needles above me.

There's a smell of damp earth after rain. A small clear stream is running nearby. There's distant bird song from high in the trees.

A grass snake rustles by through the leaf piles. A red squirrel runs up a nearby tree.

The trees are old and straight and very tall.

I come upon five stone steps going down to a deeper part of the forest.

They are worn from the treading of many feet, and many rains and many seasons.

At the bottom of the steps is a small clearing.

I stand
looking around
wood mice scurry past
it's very quiet
still, and shady

Ahead of me there's a tree with a long groove in the bark, a deep mossed hollow.

As I look, it seems to open, the bark peeling back. A man steps out. He smiles.

he holds out his hands
to me and says *come*
I step into his arms
and rest my head
on his chest

He has long grey-brown hair, the colour of the bark, and skin the colour of summer dusk.

His clothes are the colour of autumn leaves. He has brown sandals on his feet.

I can hear his heart beating where my head rests. It is slow and the beats are long and deep.

when he speaks
his voice is like
distant rumbling thunder

I know that he knows all that there is to know, and more.

I ask him the one question that has puzzled me all my life.

I say — *is there a God?*

he laughs
it's like the sound
of a great waterfall
landing on rocks
far below

Listen, he says, *the answer is this —*

Everything is God. God is Everything.

He lets go of me and turns away. I don't want him to go.
He moves back into the tree and the bark folds around him
and he is gone.

I sit on the bottom step and cry for a time.

Then I go back up the steps, along the worn path, and
back to my home.

> there is dust
> everywhere
> as if my house
> has been empty
> a long long time

My face is sticky with tears and cobwebs.
With my finger I write on the old dining table in the
thick dust—

Everything is God, God is Everything

and I wake in my own bed, in my strange, clean house.

the rutted road

the intruder

way up high
on the cathedral spire
the falcons sleep
as I do in my house
on the busy street below

The story of the wild peregrine falcons in the nest box high on Norwich Cathedral spire is a strange one, a soap opera, and people around the globe have followed it on the webcam installed by the nest.

We have watched the two adult falcons nesting there for 5 years (falcons mate for life) happily raising brood after brood of healthy chicks.

This year began the same way. Four chicks hatched from the eggs and were doing fine, fed by both male and female parent birds.

All four were females this time (perhaps due to the aging of the male bird, at the end of his lifespan), and therein lay the problem.

A yearling falcon from Bath, another Cathedral city, flew hundreds of miles looking for a mate (male falcons are sparse in England) and happened on Norwich.

She was a strong bird with a drive for procreation. She attacked the mother bird and drove her away. The mother was later found dead of her injuries.

Then the Intruder waited, harassing the young birds as they grew. They learned to drop low on the nest floor in a huddle and keep silent until she passed by. The male parent bird fed the chicks — an amazing job for a lone dad. He wore himself out, growing thin and stressed and no doubt missing his lifelong mate.

One by one the chicks grew big enough to fledge. And as they did, one by one the Intruder attacked. There were to be no other females on her new territory.

The male falcon brought her kills, hoping to appease her. But still, as the chicks flew, she attacked.

down the road
the church bells ring
for matins
the smallest falcon
flies first

in some kind
of strange bird ritual
it touches beaks
with its siblings
and takes to the sky

It soon lay wounded on the ground, and died.

again and again
the predator dives
the chicks freeze
playing dead . . . outsmarted
the intruder leaves

soon the chicks
must leave the safe nest
and one by one
as they take flight
the Intruder attacks

The second, a stronger bird, was badly wounded but managed to fly to a hiding place in the tower. The same with the third.

Alone, the last chick sat on the edge of the nest, calling and calling. That was her downfall. The Intruder swooped and knocked her to the ground.

She died in a flash of wings.

> how many tears
> have I shed
> for these birds
> killed and wounded
> as soon as they fly?

Now the Trust, whose policy is usually not to interfere with nature, bowed to public demand and they caught the wounded chicks and took them to a sanctuary where vets did surgery on broken wings and legs and stitched wounds. As the chicks recovered they began to feed and fly and grow strong again. They will be taught to hunt and will be released into the 'wilds' of Norfolk some weeks hence. Whether they will survive is still questionable. Such a start in life is not easily overcome.

And the homing instinct may take them back to the Cathedral grounds and back into the danger of the claws of the Intruder.

As for her . . . well, her drive to find a mate and the killing it led her to do, does not so far have any happy ending.

The old male falcon seems uninterested which is hardly surprising.

The female has hollowed her nest in the box high on the spire and sits on the edge calling.

Joy McCall

In the end she goes to hunt her own food and comes back with her kills (small birds) to the empty nest.

Well, we could say that birds do not feel as people do and the male will soon forget the slaughter of his mate and chicks — but I'm not so sure.

I think there is the same instinct, the same feeling in all creatures. Love is love.

Humankind reasons and thinks, but our basic instincts are just the same as those falcons, to mate, to bond, to care for our young.

It has been a sad thing to watch the story unfold. And yet, I feel sorry for the Intruder whose battle seems to have been in vain. I wonder where she will go, now?

she sits calling
night and day
on the edge
of the cold nest
and still, he does not come . . .

If you would like to know more about the Norwich Cathedral falcons, visit this website: https://hawkandowltrust.org/web-cam-live/norwich-cathedral-side

all day

Joy McCall

Friend, you wish to know the identity of the Beloved,
The name of true love. But don't you know already?
Each journey taken arrives at the same place : Home.

Don Wentworth, from ghazal: All Day

> I have been lost
> since the first crash
> wandering
> in strange villages
> with no streetlights
>
> the houses
> are dark and shuttered
> the doors all locked
> I go knocking
> no one answers
>
> the church
> is padlocked
> no candles burning
> the organ is silent
> the font is dry

Joy McCall

the school is closed
the swings are gone
from the playground
empty tankards
lie by the pub door

there are sheep
roaming on the hill
a cuckoo calls
I am weeping,
picking wild blackberries

blue ice

*Today, like every other day, we wake up empty and
frightened. Don't open the door to the study
and begin reading. Take down the dulcimer. Let the beauty
we love be what we do. There are hundreds of ways to kneel
and kiss the ground.*

Jalal ad-Din Rumi

> there are symphonies
> rising up in concert halls
> and there are small songs
> that barely fly, but hover
> and touch my face like a kiss

I begged the gods – may I have one day without pain?
They replied – what will you give?

I did not know and so I asked them – what should I pay?
I was too late – they had already gone.

> everything changes
> the earth shifts on its axis
> polar ice melts
> the seas rise over the land
> I am overcome by fear

Life is like an ice floe, breaking away from the shore,
melting, shifting, drifting – as Leonard Cohen sang in
'Anthem,' – *there's a crack in everything.*

> my head is a mess
> there are strange silences
> amid the bedlam
> of shaky voices rising
> from my once-solid sense of self

In the quiet of the night I think of the Inuit –
the old suffering ones who went onto the ice
to lay down and wait for death.

> I thought that hell
> would be more like blazing fire
> but it is white ice . . .
> for me the frozen wastelands
> my days fall like winter snow

> when the thaw comes
> I will be far from home
> from sheltering walls
> from the potatoes baking
> and the heater's orange glow

> where will be the arms
> that hold me safe then?
> he will be waiting
> his heart beating,
> and though I call, he may not hear

What lies between us has not yet taken shape. The ice is
shifting, starting to sing the blue song
of separation and loss.

I am not ready . . .
I fight the leaf fall, the dark
I watch for the sun
rising later in the day
setting early in the dusk

all the ways I find
to look at death and dying
chop and change and turn
from one thing to another
like watercolours, running

The country man sings *
let the picture paint itself
it'll be alright
I cry back — *it is not so*
the canvas is chaotic

I see no painting, no red, yellow, green; only the cold blues,
the pale periwinkle, the twilight indigo.

what is this pain?
shards from the ice floe
stabbing and melting
into my flesh, bringing
the slow chill of despair

hold me closer, love
pull me back onto the land
must I leave this life?
too dear are the fields, the hedges
the singing of birds

87

Joy McCall

I bargain with the gods for more weeks. months, years but
they do not care — what is one woman's life among so many?

I lay in my bed; rest and sleep do not come, my body fights
itself and how can my mind make any sense of it all?

a day will come
when I understand
and make my own peace
with cold blue endings
but not yet — I am adrift

Rodney Crowell

wormwood and gall

Facing some difficult medical choices, I turned to the Tarot and drew the card of the Tower – bodies falling from a building on fire.

That didn't help so I tried the Zen cards and the I Ching and got The Fool.

Then I did what I often do and took my father's worn old King James Bible and closed my eyes and opened it – Lamentations 3.

I debated He with a capital H but it seemed wrong to blame God for everything.

I'm sure it's not his fault my skin is old and my bones are broken. And it was an olive pit that broke my tooth, not gravel stones.

he hath led me
and brought me
into darkness
but not into light
against me is he turned

my flesh
and my skin
hath he made old
he hath broken
my bones

Joy McCall

he compassed me
with travail
and hath set me
in dark places
as they that be dead of old

he hath
hedged me about
that I cannot get out
he hath made
my chain heavy

he hath
enclosed my ways
with hewn stone
he hath made
my paths crooked

he was unto me
as a bear
lying in wait
and as a lion
in secret places

he hath filled me
with bitterness
he hath made me
drunken
with wormwood

he hath also
broken my teeth
with gravel stones
he hath covered me
with ashes

I said, my strength
and my hope is perished
remembering mine affliction
and my misery —
the wormwood and the gall

Lamentations 3 King James Bible

there are no answers
to my questions
the taste of absinthe is bitter
my joints are stuck
with seed pearl and gall

falling

the choice
between the devil
and the deep blue sea
between the fires of pain
or the drugging of opiates

I am torn as to which to choose. One seems as bad as the other.

The neurology clinic, where the kindest of doctors did his work, was among lovely woods, and so I wrote —

falling

while I wept
with pain and fear
the yellow
maple leaves
kept falling

and later
I sat under
the willows
while a swan drifted
down the river

and the ducks
all slept on the bank
their heads
under their wings
and made small noises

and the day
passed and came
to its end
and I was glad
and sorry

and I slept on
through the morning
into the day
and dreamed I fell slowly
a red, dead leaf

barley

in the dream
I'm walking through a field
of ripe barley
small mice are running
through the stalks

half of the field has been harvested
there are great piles of cut barley ready to be gathered in

a man standing among the uncut crop is calling my name
he is wearing a dark brown hooded cloak

not the reaper although he has been scything
he has a kind face long straggly hair under the hood

as I draw near
he is tapping his watch
— *you're late*
I stand listening to the wind
rustling the barley

the man folds
his arms across his chest
and smiles
not yet then he says
not yet

graves

In the faded old photograph, taken the year I was born, my father in his long white Royal Air Force Chaplain's robes stands praying in a field in Burma.

There's a crowd of villagers in rough clothes gathered at the edge of the field.

Around my father, Indian soldiers stand to attention in simple khaki uniforms with pale belts.

The soldiers have spent much of the hot day digging shallow graves for their fallen comrades, one grave after another, until the field is full of graves.

My English father begins to pray the formal prayer to his God for the peace of the souls of the dead —

Oh God
whose mercies
cannot be numbered
accept these prayers
for these thy servants ...

Many of the soldiers do not understand his words or his strange faith.

They bow their heads and pray their own prayers to Brahma, Vishnu and Shiva, and others of their gods —

his body is gone
may his soul find its way
to his true nature
moving ever closer
to the One God . . .

When the war ends, my father comes home, bringing the photograph, his heart heavy with death.

I am a small girl
lying in my bed
listening
as my father weeps
below the stairs

how can I sleep
when I hear too
the guns, the cries?
in my dreams
I see dead bodies

Even when he was old and dying, my father kept the photograph with him.

He spoke often of the war and the sounds of death and his own inner battle to hold onto his faith.

It was never easy, he said, but he did it. It was his calling.

He said that not everyone is lucky enough to have a life filled with meaning and purpose, as he did.

if I was in a field
full of the war dead
my faith would fly
with all that breath . . .
gone with the wind

truck

I'm watching the news. A dark-skinned man is standing, looking into the back of an open truck.

In it are piles of canvas sacks, covering the bodies of 33 children killed in an air strike while going to school in their bus.

A soldier is pulling back the sacks to show the faces.

The man starts sobbing, broken . . .

Yusef
Mohammed
Ali—
my sons
my sons

He falls to the ground and begin to wail and weep.

for a man
looking at his children
lying dead
there can be
no comfort

Men stand around the truck, breaking, unable to grasp the horror.

the bombs that fell
were made in England
in my land . . .
innocent of it
yet I feel a heavy guilt

the wheels of trade
keep on turning
careless
money changes hands
there is work for men

dead children
broken fathers
corruption
what is this world
we are making?

weeping
I watch a bee
on a flower
I touch a mossy stone —
I don't know what else to do

Armistice Day 2018

In Flanders fields the poppies blow
Between the crosses, row on row . . .

– Lieutenant-Colonel John McCrae, 1915

> beside my river
> rows of paper poppies
> red as blood . . .
> when the night rains come
> they too will fade, and fall

recipe

be wary
of the untouchable
the dark sloe
her black thorns
bring easy blood

After the first winter frost, take a long thorn from the prunus tree to pick and gather the softening dark purple fruit into a glass bottle. Do not touch the berries; they will ruin.

the scent
of the white flower
goes to the head
the hours pass in a daze
the petals fall

Do not remove the stones from the fruit, they will bring the taste of almond nuts.
Add a teacupful of raw coarse brown sugar.

the cold days come
all men are fools
the berry
must fall to the ground
the skin bears bruises

Fill the bottle with good gin. Speak your thanks to the juniper tree.

Grind fresh cloves and cinnamon and add to the pale liquid.

> *communis*
> the juniper, the sloe
> common trees
> they bathe like sluts
> in the mud-puddles

Put the bottle in a dark place. Wait. And wait. At least until the next summer.

When the gin is ruby-red, pour it through a muslin cloth and back into the bottle.

Add a new cork. Write the date on the glass.

Take the sediment and stones back to the hedges to feed the roots.

Remember to touch the bark while you hum the gin-song. If you don't know it, make up your own.

> how quickly
> the bottle is empty
> the year is gone
> the roots mutter and plot
> death in the deep earth

Do not go gin-drunk into the streets. You will be beaten and robbed. You may die.

Sophie

new year's night
music and fireworks . . .
and far out at sea
a young girl
is drifting on the tide

a storm is brewing
the wind whips up the waves
the moon is full
the ships are at anchor
in Yarmouth harbour

the rowdy sailors
are drinking to the new year
in the old pub
there's life and hope
on the dry land

the sea
is vast, deep and cold
the girl is so small
and is this
what she wanted?

it's not right
for one so young
to be in the sea
let the tide take her to shore . . .
let her mother cover her face

Even the local crooks and their kids are out every day
searching the shore for any signs of Sophie, but so far —
nothing.

Mary

There are some memories that stay with me, others that fade, only to return years or decades later.

Some I put to the back of my mind because they were troubling—and then something happens later to remind me of them.

So it was with the old lady in Room 23 in the Church of England Home, long ago.

She was a lady who said little and didn't seem to want to make friends. I often asked her if she was all right. She would say, 'Yes, I like my own company best.'

I learned
from many old folk
down the years
how to be true
to my own self

The lady, Mary, had been put in the Home by her son Bill, who did not know how to take care of her, and thought it best.

He was a good son, who visited every Sunday, and sat with her through the services in the little chapel, and had lunch with her in the dining hall.

I asked Mary
about her only son —
'a good boy;
he was a good boy
from the day he was born'

She seemed content enough. On warm days she sat in the garden. When it grew cold and dark, she sat a corner of the lounge reading her Bible.

Sometimes she would slip into the chapel and quietly play the piano — always old hymns like Amazing Grace and It is Well with my Soul.

She was no trouble to the staff . . . but somehow . . .

a woman who is
never troublesome
is a worry —
what is she thinking?
what burden does she carry?

The memory of that one day has come back to me, out of the blue.

I came to work early as always, that Sunday. The night nurse gave me her report — all was well.

I began my rounds. Patients were starting to get up and dressed.

room 23
was silent
I knocked gently
on the door
no one answered

The room was chilly and dark. I pulled back the curtains saying, 'Good morning Mary. You're sleeping late today.'

I turned to the bed —

she lay
under the covers
not moving
a heavy plastic bag
tied over her head

For a moment, I froze, then I moved to undo the tie from around her neck and pulled off the bag, and turned on the light.

her skin was cold
she had no pulse
no heartbeat —
Mary had been dead
for some time

The doctor came and certified death. The coroner came and interviewed staff.

Her son came for his regular Sunday visit. I took him to my office and told him his mother had passed away. He sat down, shaking.

'I should have known, and called you,' he said. 'I got a letter from her on Friday that just said, 'With love, Mother,' with a small thin key taped to the letter.'

We went to her room. I asked if he wanted to see her — the staff had carefully covered her white face with a white sheet.

'Not yet,' he said.

he looked
around the room
his eyes searching —
a simple wooden box
sat on her table

Of course, the key fit. He opened the box, neither of us
knowing what to expect.

It was stuffed full with faded letters in their envelopes.
He began to read them and passed me one.

a letter
in blue ink
of love
and longing
and sorrow

We looked at the posting dates. The letters were written
over forty years, from when Mary was about 30 until she was
over 70, then they ended.

They were posted from Exmouth, Devon. And there we
were in Norwich, Norfolk.

Her son sat down, bemused. The letters were all signed,
William, and began 'my dearest Mary'.

'I don't understand', he said — 'My father's name was
George Henry. Who is this William?'

He went to the bed and pulled back the sheet and looked
at his mother's face — the mother he thought he knew.

he began to weep
kneeling with his head
on her cold hand
and spoke —
'Mother, why didn't you tell me?'

That is all I really know of the story of Mary and her son Bill.

The coroner ruled it suicide. Mary's son took the box and the letters home.

We met a few times, the last time at the funeral and blessing.

He said he had tried to trace William without luck, and thought he must be dead.

Life went on at the Home. Patients died as very old people do, and others took their places.

Mary was just one more name on the records.

I moved on to other work, other patients, other challenges.

why now
do I remember Mary?
it is almost Christmas —
on the radio the carol plays
Mary did you know?

Mary did you know that your baby boy will give sight to a blind man?

Mary did you know that your baby boy will calm a storm with his hand?

Did you know that your baby boy has walked where angels trod?

When you kiss your little baby, you kiss the face of God.

Mark Lowry

I grow older
and remember Mary
and wonder —
did she die, in the end,
because of love?

please to remember the fifth of November, gunpowder, treason, and plot

for Brian Zimmer, again

Every year now it's the same on this night — all over my city people are partying at bonfires, fireworks are flashing up into the night sky, and I think of my dear friend who lost hope, lost the light, and could stay no longer.

Guy Fawkes night
and all through the dark
the sounds of fireworks
while in my head
his low sad voice reading

— and he would sing, in the evenings as we talked on the phone, his own quiet evensong psalms —

blessed is he
that considereth the poor
the Lord
will deliver him
in time of trouble

the Lord
will strengthen him
upon the bed of languishing
and wilt make all his bed
in his sickness

mine own familiar friend
in whom I trusted
which did eat of my bread
hath lifted up his heel
against me

as for me
thou upholdest me
in mine integrity
and settest me
before thy face for ever

found tanka from Brian's much-loved Psalm 41, King James
Bible.

he has peace
and I am glad of it
and yet, and yet . . .
the dark empty space
he left behind him

freeze the arrow in the air

There were those on the Scottish isles who told the true stories of the longships and the Viking invaders; the long bows, the battleaxes, the broadswords; the raping, the pillaging; the slaughter.

And later Orkney islanders, the descendants of Vikings, wrote poems and tales of that history.

it was not all
blood and thunder
broken arrows
broken bodies
the smell of death

There were times when the ships came with music and singing and gifts and the handshake of friendship.

Then the poet-heralds in the bows of the ships told no tales of slaughter and death —

they sang the songs
of the great journeys
the sails, the oars
the sight of the shores
of the beautiful land

old island men
part Viking, part Scots
sit around the pub fires
drinking rough ale
retelling the tales

There was one man, a little mad, often drunk, who wrote the stories in ways that would chill the blood.

His name was George Mackay Brown and when he died, his name lived on and on in those islands, and over the hills and far away.

And a young man, in Scandinavia, read the tales and sang the song of one ship that came in peace.

He is a Dane, with long red hair and a great red beard, tall and strong, with a voice that would melt the northern ice.

A thousand years and as many miles from those longships and battle axes and poet-heralds, he sings —

freeze the arrow in the air
make your mark and leave it
hanging there
be the first to turn around
take the leap . . .to higher ground

Rasmussen

I heard him singing, and I wept and I thought of Sven, and the islands, and battles, and struggles, and old poems . . . and choices.

And I wished men now would learn those same lessons and bring gifts and songs instead of war.

Jarrod

I'm talking on the phone to British Gas to arrange a boiler service. A young lad called Jarrod is talking me through all the bureaucratic stuff, as they must. He has a strong Scottish accent. I ask him where he comes from. He says Eastwick, a little village outside Gretna Green where the famous blacksmith's forge stands, a place of marriages since ancient times, and the place my own marriage to Andy was blessed.

> the blacksmiths stood
> down the centuries
> speaking the words
> joining the elopers
> 'over the anvil'

Scotland had its own wedding rules and people came from other countries to cross the border for the freedom to marry for love.

I asked Jarrod what he was doing far south of the border, in Leicester. He explained that he could not find a job he could do in his native land, so he came south for work. I asked how he liked it all.

He said,

I love my work
I hate Leicester
every day
I long to go north . . .
to go home

in my village
I knew everyone
everyone knew me
there is such comfort
in familiarity

He sounded sad. I asked if he could not go home again?

the Scots are tribal
there are the clans
the strong sense
of being apart
from the mainland

He said,

I would love to go home
there is no work for me there
and a man
is not a real man
unless he earns his pay

115

I felt sad for him. I felt the same for the lad from the Welsh Valleys who had to move to London to find any work when the mines all closed.

the outskirts
can be barren places
without hope
for young men —
maybe it was always so

I asked Jarrod if there was nothing he could do for work, at home? He was quiet a long time. Then he said, 'I will speak to my boss about opening a call centre in Scotland, and I will run it, because I can; I'm good at my job.'

We spoke then of the borderlands where I grew up, and where fifty years later, he grew up, just on the other side of Hadrian's Wall.

We talked of the border reivers of long ago. He would have liked to be one of them.

He arranged me a boiler service. He added me to a priority list so that anyone disabled can get quick help with heating and lighting problems.

I wept then
feeling the care
of a stranger
on a call-phone
far away

Something had changed in just a few minutes, on both ends of that phone line.

little things
everyday things
open doors . . .
a few words
an open heart

way stations

Wandering Down the Lane

torn scraps
of old brown paper
litter the floor
of the church ruins —
who was here?

I never know what I'm going to find when I go along the
lane to the 11th century ruin in the graveyard of the 13th
century still-used church; sometimes condoms and needles,
sometimes bottles (the ancient pub is also in the church
graveyard, and used to be the priest's ale store); I haven't
found a body . . . yet. I go to say my solitary prayers in the
ruins. Sometimes I light a candle in the open church.

Tombland

It is not just the living that are frequent visitors to the cobbled streets of old Norwich . . .

Situated at one end of Tombland are The Maids Head Hotel and Samson & Hercules House. Both have ghost stories associated with them, and when you explore their heritage a little further it is perhaps easy to understand why. The Maids Head dates back to the 13th century, when it was called the 'Murtle Fish'. The name was changed following a visit by Queen Elizabeth I to Norwich in 1578. Like most places visited by the Royal Party in 1578, the Black Death or Plague was destined to follow in its wake. A member of the large party spread the plague as they travelled from place to place and Norwich was no exception.

From August 1578 to February 1579 almost 5000 victims of the plague were recorded in the city. In total almost half the entire population of Norwich perished from the Plague during this time. While rats thrived in the narrow alleyways, the grim cry of 'bring out your dead' rang throughout the city. As the number of bodies grew in colossal number, formal burials were abandoned in favour of mass-graves or 'plague pits'. Cartloads of bodies were taken to the Cathedral Close, which became a large burial area. The graveyards behind St. George's church are so high as they were raised to accommodate the huge number of bodies.

The church played an even more sinister role during this time, being the site where opportunistic looters of the dead and dying were taken if caught. After being bound at the ankles and wrists, they would be dropped headfirst from St. George's church onto the unforgiving ground below. Their bodies, whether dead or still alive, would then join the plague victims in the lime-filled pits.

One of the largest plague pits in Norwich was dug below the Tombland church of St. George. This grim feature, along with the close proximity to the Cathedral, may be the root cause of numerous tales of hauntings and disturbances in the building throughout the years. These include the ghost of a young girl who apparently starved to death in Augustine Steward House next door after it was boarded up during the plague, spectral monks, shadowy figures and recurring nightmares for worshippers of being buried alive in a huge pit full of dead bodies . . .

lost

around the corner
from the all-night bars,
an old church —
cobblestones pave the way
to untended graves

damp and cool
and musty, inside
a woman sits —
dim light filters
through grimy windows

distant thump
of music, and clubbers
shouting and singing —
the woman lifts her head,
her prayers disturbed

Joy McCall

on the hard pew
she settles to sleep,
shivering —
rain begins to fall
rats scratch behind the altar

below the nave
thick lime in the pit
shifts a little —
then closes again
over nameless small corpses

winter lamp

a winter evening
and again in the attic window
of the derelict house
an oil lamp shines
on a boy's face

His parents died in the house years ago, while he was at university, and I don't know if he is real or a spirit. But the lamplight is real.

who is Sylvia?

we were sitting in the cedar gateway singing, when
Sylvia dressed in a long brown and dark red patterned gown
and tight brown boots came up from the ground and came to
us (drifting, as ghosts do) and spoke in such a quiet old-
fashioned kind of country voice:

thank you
on behalf of all the others
for the songs you sing
and then she danced a little
swirling her skirts

she danced
across the browning grass
and went into the earth again –
and all was still and quiet
in the graveyard

I don't believe in ghosts . . . do I?

Poppy

Our pub landlady was expecting twins but sadly one died early in the pregnancy. The doctors recommended aborting both little ones, but the landlady is made of strong stuff. She chose to carry on to full term, carrying one living babe and one dead one. She wanted the dead one to be allowed a proper burial, and not to be thrown in an incinerator, as is usual.

It was hard for her, knowing.

still —

she sat behind the bar
every day till closing time
filling the glasses
with ale and cider
joking and smiling

When the time came, the two babes were born and the dead one had the good burial her mother and father wanted.

They chose not to tell the living one about her twin until she was much older, but when I sat by the pub fire —

the little one
sat on my lap
and whispered in my ear
don't tell, but
my sister is here

Time passed and school time came and the little girl struggled. She would faint in class and in the playground. The doctor sent her to see a heart specialist who gave them grave news — her heart was in bad shape.

the small girl
who shared the womb
with her dead twin
sees the cardiologist
for her broken heart

next time I see her
she hugs me and says
my sister says
my heart has to beat
for the two of us now

I go to the ruined church near the pub and pray that her heart will keep on beating, steady and true.

gravestones, pot and a husky dog

On what would have been my mother's 98th birthday, we went to the cemetery, and in the cold rain under dark grey skies, we sang 'Happy Birthday' to her.

> her name
> carved with my father's
> makes no sense
> I still hear them
> laughing, praying, singing

We laid a Norfolk flint hagstone on the base of her headstone, to keep the witches away; not that witches would frighten the bones of such a good mother. She would have just smiled at them and put the kettle on for tea.

There were rabbit droppings on the grass of her grave. She would love that. She loved all creatures.

An English robin was singing, high in an ivy-covered oak tree.

The cemetery holds many hundreds of graves, some centuries old.

There are equally ancient trees, mostly evergreen except for the wide-spreading oaks.

Like all graveyards, there are great dark yew trees to keep out the cattle and the black witches.

spruce and pine
Norway fir
a cypress
beautiful and graceful
and the necessary yews

amid the disorder
of headstones
angels and crosses . . .
a plain hundred all the same
young men, killed in war

So many of the stones had the same words repeated
again and again —

rest in peace
together again
dearly beloved
in heaven
. . . gone home

The little pathways between the stones were narrowed
with grasses and moss, barely wide enough for my
wheelchair.

three rough lads
leaning on a crypt
smoking pot
I breathed deep
and smiled as I passed

I guess they were playing hooky from school — and who
would think to look for them in a cemetery?
Further along the path a young man was walking a
gorgeous husky dog. We could see the wolf in its face and

thick silver fur. A rare kind of dog in this place of small Norfolk and Norwich terriers.

We stopped to talk. The young man told his story, of being crippled and lost and alone and broke.

He had tried to hang himself from a tree, but was found and cut down.

He spoke of a lifetime of mental illness and alienation and wanting to die. Then he had seen the dog in a rescue place.

The dog had been there a long time, too big for homing and miserable, unhealthy, as a working dog would be in a cage.

The man took the dog home with him to his bare flat.

He got books about huskies. He could not walk the dog enough with his damaged legs.

He found an old three-wheeled bike and fixed reins to it and every day the husky pulled him through miles of quiet Norfolk lanes, far from his small flat, summer and winter alike. He said the dog was happy. By the wagging of its tail, I think he was right.

The young man said that he went at the end of each day to the old market just as the stalls were closing, and bought for a few pennies(all he had) the leftover fish and chicken from the day's sales. He knew what a husky dog liked to eat. They shared their supper.

the husky
stood still at his side
the young man said
he saved my life
I saved his

There is always sadness in the air of a cemetery. That day there was also gladness. And life, among all the death.

131

Salvation Army

Every weekend the Salvation Army not only marches with brass bands through English city streets, playing hymns and sacred songs; but they also take their mobile food vans out to where the hungry and homeless gather, to give them hot meals and cups of tea; and they wash the feet of the homeless ones, as they believe their Lord did, and would want them to do too.

I don't know what I believe about religion, but I admire that devotion.

This Sunday I met an old woman in the uniform; she was waiting for a bus to the city centre, and carrying a bucket.

the old woman kneels
washing with arthritic hands
dirty feet
ulcerated feet
weary, smelly feet

she listens
as she has for decades
to the stories
of the addicts, the drunks
the ill, the lost souls

she says little
she is busy washing
listening
giving loving care
the best way she knows

when she goes home
exhausted, aching,
she prays a while
takes a bath, eats her supper
and falls asleep by the fire

she wakes in the night
shivering, the fire dead
and praying her thanks
she climbs the stairs
to her own single bed

talking to the dead

for Larry

I was telling a friend about pain and doctors and their concerns for my future. I was crying and afraid, not knowing what choice I should make about surgery and medications. Then my friend said — *find someone dead who you have known well, and talk to them.*

I laughed. I thought a long while about that. Whether we believe in an afterlife or not, we can still talk to the dead as we did when they lived; the way we can talk to an acorn, not knowing if it will ever be an oak tree.

So —

I went to Gogo-an
to the old hermit's hut
but Ryokan
had no answers for me
his life nothing like mine

There were no noisy hospitals, many stories high, in his day.

I sought out Sven
and spoke some Swedish
to my grandfather
he was silent
and gone, far away

134

I tried some of the poets I have read for many decades —
Hughes and Frost and Cornford — and although I could
sense them, all I heard them say were lines of poems from
the pages of their books.

I found an old priest
I knew so well —
he said nothing
but bowed his head
and went on praying

even the dear poet
who took his own life
was silent
busy writing words
on a white page

Sam Hamill
did look at me
with serious eyes
he is not long
in his cold grave

But he spoke nothing.

My mother is resting in peace. I will not wake her. Her
long life is done, rightly so.

In my head I go through the names of those I have
known and loved. None of it seems right. Somehow, dead is
dead. When the ties are cut, they stay cut and should not be
tied together again.

I held a small stone
grey and smooth
in my hand
my fingers curled
around it

I held it to my cheek
and I spoke many words
over many hours
and they sank
inside the stone

I grew tired. Morning came. In my hand was a small grey
stone. I laid it back with all the others in the garden. It may
seem crazy to talk to a stone (although Charles Simic did)
but the stones in these fields are flint and come from the
bones of long-dead fish.

they know
the weight of the ocean
the cold and the dark
the loneliness
of the seabed

I learn slowly
and stupidly
how it will be
in a thousand years
when I too am stone

asylum

There is an old abandoned asylum on the outskirts of Norwich. It has been standing empty for decades.

a rambling house
covered in ivy
hidden
in brambles and briars
all the chimneys fallen

Once, it was a busy place where lunatics lived out their lives together, working in the gardens growing their food, and in the orchards gathering fruit, in the kitchens, cooking and bottling, on the wards making beds, and in the laundry washing the dirty clothes and sheets by hand.

Despite the madness, it was not a bad place, as some institutions were back then. The inmates were treated well and made to feel useful.

When World War 1 came, many of the workers went to serve their country and other helpers came in to take care of the place.

it was a time
of unrest then
strange faces
strange ways
the madmen uneasy

Some of the workers were killed in the war. Those who came back were changed, but still, their faces were familiar and things slowly got back to what passed as normal.

There are small plaques on the wall of the asylum with the names and jobs of those who did not return. To read them, you must climb through the overgrowth and carry some rag to wipe the brass and read the names.

Frederick

the doctor
who brought help
to so many
could not save himself —
he is bones, somewhere

Samuel

the gardener
who sang as he worked
among the roses —
they still bloom
among the tangling weeds

Harry

the dispenser
of old medicines
for peace
and quiet sleep —
now he rests in peace

Thomas

the tailor
who patched, mended
made hems —
they sewed his wounds
to no avail

Joe

the cobbler
maker of good shoes
re-soling, re-heeling —
his own feet and legs
blown away by shells

Soon, the old building will be taken down to make way
for new housing which is badly needed.

The big books of written records of names of inmates
will be stored in the castle dungeons. The brass plaques that
carry the names of the war dead will be moved to a stone in
the cemetery at the edge of the gardens where inmates were
buried.

The small chapel there will be demolished but its tower
will remain standing as all church towers must in Norfolk. It
is a sin and against the law to remove the towers that carried
the prayers of the faithful up to God. There's comfort in
seeing the lonely towers dotted across this small county —
650 of them.

our ancestors
had faith and hope
now both
are slipping away . . .
still, there is love

And now abideth faith, hope, love, these three; but the greatest of these is love.

I Corinthians, 13:13 King James Bible

faithful

I have worked in many places as a nurse and remember so many patients with admiration and often amazement and great respect for the human spirit.

At this time of year I think of an old lady called Mrs Dorothy Downes. She was a Methodist, and despite all kinds of hardships, she never lost faith in her God.

When I knew her, she was ninety, her husband long dead. She had four children who visited her every week. A happy family.

During the next three years, one by one, her children died. First, her daughter, of cancer. Then her youngest son, of a sudden stroke.

Then another son in a car crash; he lived a month on life support, then died.

It was at this time of year that we would have a big Christmas dinner for the old folks and their families.

Mrs Downs was sombre, but glad that she would have her oldest, precious first-born son Derek with her.

The evening before the party, I got a call to say Derek had had a heart attack and passed away.

I went to her room and I sat and told her. It was one of the saddest moments of my life.

the old one
sat alone and sad
her faith was shaken
and she prayed
please God, take me, too

She spent that Christmas alone in her room, and every day afterwards. We brought her food and drink and helped her to bath and bed.

I would give her
toast and tea
and a hug
she took all three
with a sad grace

she would look at me
and quote some verse
from her Bible
as she always did
but she never smiled

She lived another year after that, going through the days, trying to keep the faith.

I'm guessing that she was glad when her quiet end came.

When I saw her in the coffin, the undertaker had put a smile on her face, as they usually do.

I asked him
to take it away
let her go
honestly
to her God

I'm hoping that the last thing she heard when her life ended was her God, saying – *well done, thou good and faithful servant.*

desert sands

My uncle, well over 90, was long retired from his holy work as the Canon of Gloucester Cathedral. His dear wife had died after almost 70 years of marriage. He decided to follow his lifelong dream. He booked a ticket for a cruise down the Nile.

in his old Bible
were many tales
of the vast desert sands
nothing like the small sands
on the English shores

The cruise ship sailed on and on. He saw the pyramids. He saw the great sphinx. He saw many ancient cities. It was all like a dream to the old man.

After many days and nights of travel, the cruise ship stopped at anchor in a bay by a town surrounded by desert. It was the turning point. One day there and the ship would turn for home. Smaller boats ferried the passengers to the harbour.

The town was noisy and the market place was wild with smells and sounds and sights and the unfamiliar language. My uncle wandered through, not finding what he sought. There were Bedouin men at the edge of the town offering camel rides.

That was it. My uncle paid, and was lifted up onto the
camel. His bag was tied at his back. The group set off across
the sands.

My uncle had had surgery for cancer years before. He
had urostomy and colostomy. He was arthritic. And he was
old. But still . . . there was the dream, overriding it all.

his heart
grew so happy
that he sang
high on the camel,
loud hymns to his God

The Bedouins smiled and chanted, 'Allah, Allah' very
loudly.

They travelled a long way across the desert. The
Bedouin leader said they should turn back. My uncle paid
more money to travel on. He was busy following his dream.

'but the ship?'
said the Arab
'not yet . . .
not yet'
said my uncle

So when night came they set up camp and the men sang
their ancient poems and shared their food and drink by the
campfire . . .

". . . The tongue of a man is one half, and the other half
is his mind, and here is nothing besides these two, except
the shape of the blood and the flesh . . ." – Zuhayr, 6th
century AD

And my uncle prayed and sang his own sacred songs and went to sleep in the tent and he knew his dream was real.

> when he woke
> in the hot morning
> he thought
> 'this is not a bad place
> for an old man to die'

The tents were packed, breakfast was eaten and the camels moved on across the sands.

Meanwhile, back on the ship, my uncle was missed. The cruise had to go on. His son was called and told of his father's absence. He arranged for a smaller boat and men to go seeking the old man, fearing the worst. But when the little boat came to the stopping place, there was my uncle, somewhat the worse for wear, sitting on a rock, waiting, singing and laughing.

When he got back to England, he came to tell me his adventures. We sat in an old Norwich hotel with lunch and cups of tea.

> I was overwhelmed
> at the thought of this old
> Christian man
> riding with the Bedouin
> on a camel across the desert

I wish I had his kind of faith and courage to follow a dream like that. It was not so long afterwards that my uncle died.

Joy McCall

I wonder where he is now. I miss him. Maybe heaven is a vast desert of sand and we are given a camel at the gate.

in memory of David Charles St. Vincent Welander
(Canon Residentiary of Gloucester Cathedral and Canon Librarian)

the porch swing

I was listening to the story of Douglas in *Dandelion Wine* by Ray Bradbury, one of my favourite authors; and it came to the part where Douglas and his father were sitting on a porch swing on a summer evening, and I was thinking it would be a lovely thing to do, and I was trying to remember if I ever sat on a swing like that - and suddenly came back to me the memory of Carlisle, a grubby northern industrial town just south of the Scottish border where we moved when Grandpa Sven died, taking Granny with us. I was about 12, happy to be leaving the sexual abuse of the maths teacher but sad to be leaving my friends and the Lowestoft sea.

In the huge old Victorian sandstone vicarage there were many bedrooms and storerooms and cellars and one dark coal cellar with two rooms piled with black coal and with one tiny glassless window up near the top with a grating you could climb through, where the coalman tipped the coal deliveries. There was, left there by some previous inhabitant, who knows why, a garden swing down in the coal piles — like a porch swing. I used to go down to the cellar and swing there, all alone. It made a change from climbing to sit high in the pear tree to watch the chickens in the gooseberry patch.

I still remember
the smell of the coal
and the darkness
and the gentle comfort
of the swing

Swinging is such a primal thing. Mothers swinging children, dancers swinging around, kids on playground swings. And a short step from there to rocking horses and . . .

how we rock
our own selves
when we suffer
in body
or in mind

back and forth
humming old songs
familiar melodies
going back
in time

I think it's something I want to do more when I think of my mother so long in her grave and when my own body is failing.

Perhaps I want to be mother to myself, as we all ought to do when there's a need of comfort.

When I sat in that coal cellar on the garden swing, just a young girl, I could hear my grandmother in her room a way above, and now I wonder if she knew I was below, for she sang—

Rock my soul
in the bosom of Abraham . . .
I would not be a sinner

I'm tellin' you the reason why
I'm afraid my Lord might call me
Great God, and I wouldn't be ready to die.

Louis Armstrong

I don't think I will ever be ready to die the way my own mother was ready at the end of her days.

I think I will always *'rage against the dying of the light.' (Dylan Thomas)*, probably rocking as I rage.

the journey ends

Goeden Gollen (the Hazel Tree)

In the Welsh valleys, a long-haired man goes wandering after the wild night storm, gathering fallen sticks and twigs. He says Autumn is the best time for choosing – on the ground, the shapes of branches and sticks sing to him, clear songs of wilderness and open spaces.

> no leaves
> to mar the song
> his brown hand
> reaches down
> touching, feeling

He walks miles, the old quiver slung across his back, empty of arrows, filling with sticks that sing to him the dearest of songs.

At home, he lights the fire and sits at the heavy table with coffee, bread and cheese.

> he lays the sticks
> in rows on the table
> from large to small
> and he muses, sleepy
> as his cold hands grow warm

He smiles. He has chosen well. He gathers the sticks into the straw basket, sets the iron fire-screen on the hearth and climbs the stairs to bed.

I write to him
asking for hazelwood
small, sturdy
easy to hold
with troubled hands

It is raining hard when he wakes. He stirs up the fire,
puts on more logs and sings softly the old song —

the song
of thanks to the trees —
diolch i'r coed
rhai hardd
tan addfwyn

beautiful ones,
who bless me with logs and fire

He reads my letter, and smiles and takes a thin hazel
branch from the basket. It has deep grooves winding around
the stem where the honeysuckle grew.

deep scars
in bark and soul
from the growing
one life making its mark
upon another

He spends the day peeling the bark, carefully, as a man
does who loves his craft.

He sands gently, lovingly, not wanting to hurt the thing
made for healing.

When he is content, he takes a chunk of beeswax in his
warm hands and sings another song —

diolch
gwenyn hardd
am fel
cwyr gwenyn
yn fy nwylo

I thank you
beautiful bees
for sweet honey
and for the beeswax
here in my hands

His eyes close, he rolls and turns the stick in his hands.
The beeswax settles into the wood.
It is a meditation, a blessing to the giving tree.

while he works
he sings the songs
of the trees
and says the old prayers
of his Welsh home

Bless those minding cattle,
And those minding sheep,
And those fishing the sea
While the rest of us sleep.

May our troubles be less
And our blessings be more.
And nothing but happiness
Come through our door.
(old Welsh/Celtic blessing)

He takes the sackcloth and wipes the stick, round and around, cleaning the grooves where the honeysuckle twined.

He wraps the stick in a new pale cloth and makes the rite of candle and word —

fy ngwaith
yn falch
fynd nawr
i mewn
i un arall llaw

my glad work, go now into another hand

The postman comes to my door, and reads the label, smiling — 'Wand from the Valleys,' he says. 'I know,' I say.

Sitting by my fire, I move the wand back and forth from hand to hand. It sings to my left hand, closer to my heart.

I run my finger along the grooves where the honeysuckle grew.

what magic
is this enchantment
before I begin?
the hazel tree and its child
carry kindness

(hazel makes hedges
and walking staffs
and squirrel nuts
and deep-grooved leaves
and soft quiet songs)

I sleep well
that stormy night
I hear the sea
and dream of Bwlchtocyn *
and the hazel grove

Sometimes there is magic in the smallest of things.
Thank you, John Jones.

a small seaside village in Wales where I spent my childhood.

old boys

I was sitting by the village pond watching a moorhen nibbling duckweed. The sky was aflame in the sunset. A pale half moon rose high above the ancient church that stands crumbling on top of a bronze age burial mound.

(the moon
above the round tower
above the graveyard
above the earthen mound
above the ancient bones

the heavens
above the holy spaces
above the pews
above the worshippers
above the forgotten ancestors

the silent sky
above the solid flint
above the hymns
and the quiet prayers . . .
above the silent ground)

a couple of bicycles
leaned against a tree
the riders —
two old Norfolk boys*
sat eating pie and drinking ale

a hawk
screamed overhead
rabbits
ran for cover
into their burrows

The landlord brought me broccoli soup.

One of the old boys said — *Dew yew take care of that lass now*.

The other old boy winked and said — *Thass rare birds here today.*

A barn owl flew over the meadow with a rabbit in its claws. We watched the owl go off beyond the hill and out of sight.

The landlord said — *She'll write a poem about that, you wait; thass what she do — she write poems, about thorns and berries mostly.*

One of the old boys said — *She be better writin' poems 'out good ale and rabbit pie.*

the sun went down
behind the green hill
we said *goodbye*
godspeed to the landlord
the old boys, and the sun

One old boy said — *dew yew keep a-troshin my wumman.* **

I smiled all the way home.

> * *all men are called Boys in Norfolk. If they are past middle-age they are Old Boys.*

> ** *Norfolk people speak a strange old language. This means keep going, woman.*

159

letting go

for Jack

I went to the motorbike shop in Suffolk. I finally had the heart to take in the ancient Honda 400 Four which I have not ridden since the crash.

the old bike
like me, has been sitting
too long
it's time to say goodbye
to the bike, at least

The old mechanic will get it up and running and someone will have the joy of riding it. He falls in love with the bike at first glance, which is not surprising, she's a small beauty.

we sit
in admiration
drinking coffee
talking journeys
and engines and rides

The old guy is always sad. I haven't seen him smile in years. His only son, so mentally ill, killed his own mother a decade ago, in their home. The son is locked away forever. The old man still lives in the house where his beloved wife died.

he tells me:
her soul is there
I cannot leave her
alone in that home
we made together

he looks at the bike:
I will not sell it
I will make it good
it will stand in my workshop
shining like new

I leave behind the bike, the memories, going home wheelchair-bound; somehow feeling I have been given some kind of blessing from the old man, from the bike, from life.

once more on Barton Fell

We have spent the morning roaming the fells, picking the wild leaves, not saying much.

Each of us is looking for something we know well, unfamiliar to the other.

I hear the Gypsy a little way off, singing, 'the wild mountain thyme.'

I'm humming, 'love grows where my rosemary goes.'

The hours pass and we meet again in the old circle with our small bags of leaves and roots.

It is quiet on the hill. Just the bleating of lambs and the occasional call of a hawk.

he fills the bowl
with wild carrot
bearberry leaf
shepherd's purse
sticky goosegrass

it is now he speaks
his prayer to the land
giving thanks
for the green things
the shoots, the roots

I pass the box of matches. Somehow, a modern lighter is not right for this kind of thing.

Is there a holiness in the striking of a match? It seems so to us, a thing that goes back and back, to flint and fire.

The hawk screams and dives.

he says
what he always says
at such times —
something must die
for something else to live

The sun is low in the sky. The stones are casting long shadows. They give shelter from the chilly wind.
He strikes the match and lights the leaves. They sputter a little then settle to burn, slowly.
The smell is — what can I say — heady, bitter, beautiful, somehow fitting in this desolate place.
He is always the first to smoke. It is our habit.

the man goes ahead
making sure it is safe
for the woman —
some ancient
tribal thing

He passes the pipe and I smoke. It is like breathing in the land, the green giving of life.

We sit watching the sun going down, each lost in our own musing.
Now and then we speak, of dreams and longings and questions.

The smoking is done. What goodness there was, is within us now.

I set light to the little pile of leftover leaves and roots in a hollow in a stone. It is a hollow made by many centuries of rain and running water.

Ovid (43BC) wrote,
Dripping water hollows out stone, not through force but through persistence.

The smoke curls upwards and is caught by the wind and gone. I feel sad. Rituals do that sometimes.

my moments
like the thin smoke
there — and gone
leaving only a trace
a sea-change

all those times
I wanted to keep —
how slowly I learn
the gentle art
of letting go

oaks

Nature experts have discovered a remarkable submerged forest thousands of years old under the sea close to the Norfolk coast. The trees were part of an area known as 'Doggerland' which formed part of a much bigger area before it was flooded by the North Sea. It was once so vast that hunter-gatherers who lived in the vicinity could have walked to Germany across its land mass.

divers
just off the coast
find themselves
in an ancient forest
great oaks, and wolf bones

herring shoals
are swimming though
leafless thickets
crabs dance sideways
in twisting roots

bones
lie on the seabed
scattered
by the currents
and the tides

Joy McCall

I think
I would like my bones
to lay there
down the centuries
slowly sand-covered

I would like
fish to nibble
at my ribs
and barnacles to live
in my eye sockets

imagine
the long eternity
among the trees
with the wolves, the fish
the sand, the stones, the sea

endless ringing

for Jonathan

I have spent my life trying to grasp infinity.

I see time going on for ever ahead of me, but to imagine it forever behind me is another thing —

I think there has to be a beginning, as all the creation stories say — but what was there before that?

Can something be made of nothing?

No wonder so many philosophers went mad.

Then a wise friend said — imagine the ringing of a bell, echoing down through time, and you haven't heard the original striking of the clapper.

Suddenly past and present and future eternity makes sense. Like the mystery of the enso.

    I draw the zen card
    go with the flow
    and I see lightwaves
    hear soundwaves
    waving, infinite

    a light shines
    a bell is ringing
    the dark night is split
    there is no beginning
    there is no end

afterword

Before he died, Brian Zimmer, tanka poet and good friend of Joy's, wrote her a note:

Your poems are full of tales and lore. Readers will always gravitate toward them. They are not mere story-telling either (everyone tells stories) but bardic tales told by a master. Do you know realize how difficult it would be for me and others to intuitively choose the right detail, the color and voice for such story-telling? Chris Rea has his guitar, you have your five lines. Of course, Kei recognized from the first that you are the poet laureate of place. We have all been to Norwich.

she was known
to park her motorcycle
by stone circles
spending her nights
naming stars in five lines . . .

— Brian Zimmer, author of *Where Deer Sleep*

last word

A Life Is A Song

When the last note of the song is sung, what follows is silence.

The song is finished.

The song is completed.

The song, completed, can now find its place in the greater whole.

The song is now what the world needs it to be: finished, complete, and in its place.

Jonathan Day

Biography

Joy McCall was born in Norwich, England near the closing of World War Two. Her childhood was spent moving about in the UK, living north and south, east and west as her father was a vicar, posted to new parishes every few years.

When she was 21, after registered nurse training, she married an American and they moved to Amherst, Massachusetts.

She had two daughters with her first husband, who are the joy of her life and beautiful, inspiring women. She spent much of her adult life in Canada, working and raising her daughters. She moved back to Norwich more than thirty years ago to spend time with her aging parents and many kinfolk. She worked again as a nurse until the motorcycle crash that made her paralysed. An old man driving on the wrong side of the road . . . we never know what is around the next corner. She had planned to move back to Canada long ago but life had other plans. The snows of Canada are no place for a wheelchair-bound woman.

Joy has travelled many places in her life, biking all over the UK, following ley lines and ancient history.

She married again almost thirty years ago and has a faithful, supportive, hard-working English husband who shares her love of nature, the earth and all its creatures.

Joy has written tanka, among other kinds of poems since she was young. The old poets she reads most are Ryokan and Rumi but there are too many others to list. The encouragement of M. Kei to publish, gave her a hopeful new path to travel when life became so constrained. As Kei says 'everything is tanka.'

Joy is a Pisces and it is the bedrock of friends and family that keep the fish swimming and the river water clear.

Books by Joy McCall

Keibooks

on the cusp encore, a year of tanka
fieldgates, tanka sequences
on the cusp, a year of tanka
rising mist, fieldstones
hedgerows, tanka pentaptychs,
circling smoke, scattered bones
side by side, with Larry Kimmel

Skylark

sweetgrass and thyme
things of the edges
nogusa
Pine Winds, Autumn Rain, with Matsukaze
touching the now, with Don Wentworth
is it the wind that howls? with Liam Wilkinson
hagstones, with Claire Everett

hedgerow

singing into darkness, with Liam Wilkinson

Mousehold Publishing

Norfolk Ways, with Tim Lenton
Stillness Lies Deep, with Tim Lenton
The Beauty of Rust, with Bill Albert and Paul Levy

Printed in Great Britain
by Amazon

26637860R00106